EXCLAMATION POINTS

Other Books by Dena Taylor

*Tell Me the Number Before Infinity: the story of a girl with a
quirky mind, an eccentric family, and oh yes, a disability*
(Co-authored with Becky Taylor)

Red Flower: Rethinking Menstruation

Feminist Parenting: Struggles, Triumphs, & Comic Interludes
(Editor)

*Disabled Mothers: Stories and Scholarship
by and about Mothers with Disabilities*
(Co-edited with Gloria Filax)

Women of the 14th Moon: Writings on Menopause
(Co-edited with Amber Sumrall)

*The Time of our Lives:
Women Write on Sex after 40*
(Co-edited with Amber Sumrall)

*Sexual Harassment:
Women Speak Out*
(co-edited with Amber Sumrall)

ISBN: 978-1-944497-04-0
Library of Congress Control Number: 2020942118

Kate Hitt, Publisher, KHitt@ManyNamesPress.com (831) 728-4302
Dena Taylor, Author, (831) 588-0746

Cover © by Janet Fine, jafine@cabrillo.edu
Cover Calligraphy by Carl Rohrs
Your respect for the creator's copyright is greatly appreciated.

Some of these poems were previously published in:
Women of the 14th Moon; Tell Me the Number Before Infinity; phren-Z; Memoir (and); Writing for our Lives; Porter Gulch Review; & *The Santa Cruz Sentinel.*

EXCLAMATION POINTS

Collected Poems

by

Dena Taylor

Many Names Press
Blue Lake, California
USA

To my daughters Becky and Anna,
and grandsons Lukas and Orion—
A picture of my life

Acknowledgments

I'm forever grateful to my writing group, namely Amber Sumrall, Kim Scheiblauer, Ziggy Rendler-Bregman, Gail Brenner, Adele Shediak, Sara Walsh, and Robin Somers for their editing expertise. Huge thanks go to Kate Hitt of Many Names Press for bringing this book to light and to Janet Fine for creating the perfect cover. And to my grandson who was so excited to learn about exclamation points when he was five that I had to write a poem about it. Then when I wanted to know more about the origin of exclamation points, I found out that the first meanings were to express joy, wonderment, and emotion.

Table of Contents

Reading in Bed

Finding Crumbs

Last Eggs

Exclamation Points

Table of Contents, Continued

Perfect Timing

Holding On

Don't Forget

Reading in Bed

Reading in Bed

This word, from John Updike,

I don't recognize.

Mimetics

I look at it and squint,

a word I don't know

and can't guess

from the shape of it.

Which is how I learned to read,

by loving the shapes.

I sat on my father's chest

week after week,

as he lay on his back,

a cast spanning sternum to toes.

He would open the newspaper

and show me the beauty of words,

so before I ever went to school,

I already knew them.

I especially loved *elephant*, the tall ups

and the one hanging down.

Wordsmiths for Parents

Was there ever was a time
my mother didn't correct my language,
spoken or written?

Barely out of diapers,
on a family camping trip,
I went into the bathroom, crying
Mommy, are you in any of these?
From one of the stalls came her voice:
You mean, am I in EITHER of these!

Later, she saved my letters
written from camp
corrected with red pencil.

Dad, who wrote a sports column
for a left-wing newspaper,
was a craftsman:
You can always make it longer—
the beauty is to tighten.

He helped me write

in 25 words or less

why I liked Kellogg's Corn Flakes.

I won a Roy Rogers flashlight

but really wanted the horse.

June 19, 1953

I saw it on *60 Minutes* last night
The Rosenberg brothers, talking about their lives
Of course their name is different now

It tunneled me back to the day
their parents were executed
My family, cousins, aunts, uncles
gathered around the kitchen radio,
the room so full of sadness

I was 12, my brother Terry 10,
only slightly older
than the just-orphaned boys
I watched his bewilderment
and didn't know how I'd protect him
if this happened to us

The Basque Country

I'd always wanted to go there
long before knowing my lover.
Much longer, before I was born
my parents were passionately
anti-Franco during the
Spanish Civil War
and I grew up hearing about
the Basque people.

My brothers and I ate dinners
at Des Alpes Restaurant
in San Francisco's North Beach
where families sat at long tables
ate crunchy bread, chunky soup, meat
and the grown-ups drank red wine.

So when I looked at the photos
in the Guernica Peace Museum
I cried, remembering.

Now, I taste it all—

The fiery food and music

the wine and language

their fierceness.

Bringing Down the House

I'm uneasy, perhaps agitated
by the ghosts from the Long House
who are themselves disturbed by the demolition.
One hundred years ago this building
housed a nudist colony and much later, my family.

In the rubble was a check of my father's from 1955 for $2.60
made out to Economy Lumber. And one of my mother's
from 1967 for $14.44 to what looks like *Gem-God,*
an unlikely name for a place she'd patronize.
The word was obscured, not from ratshit and rain
but those tiny holes banks used to put in checks.

Four huge photos of my brothers and me as toddlers
had been set aside by the workers as well as a 1955 drawing
entitled "Protest against Atom War,"
more interesting than the pictures
which I'd seen before in different sizes and shades
of black and white, being a photographer's daughter.

And the gigantic mangle! Did my mother,

who never ironed anything,

win it in a *People's World* raffle,

the way my grandmother acquired her sewing machine?

I used the mangle myself as a child and what I did

to my father's shirts fits the name of the machine.

I found a painting of my uncle's also dated 1955

with big block letters on the back saying

EDA GIVE IT BACK IF YOU GET TIRED OF IT.

There was a rat-chewed copy of *Nigger* by Dick Gregory

also *David Copperfield* but nowhere was Ty Cobb's

signature that Terry got when he was ten and Dad sent him

into the field at Seals Stadium in San Francisco.

Today Maliq, the demolition guy, rests

on a box of dishes in the shade, beer in hand,

reading a book I told him he could have—

my old college copy of *Siddhartha*.

The Babysitter

I was almost 70, my brother 67

when I told him about the babysitter

who climbed into my bed

and told me to wiggle my finger

in her vagina

He remembered her too

A neighborhood teen

who showed us her breasts and bottom

I was almost seven and he was four

We didn't even consider

telling our parents

Did it *mess you up*

asked my sister-in-law with airquotes

We wondered about it and laughed

Just part of our childhood, we said

But how strange that

the memory surfaced now

when I was almost 70

and he was 67

For Sukey

You were raised by your aunt Muriel
while your mother went underground
for political reasons
I was raised by my mother
while my aunt Esther did the same

Tight as Velcro we were
before it was even invented
We learned Yiddish from your grandmother
laughed at her scolding
swam for hours in city pools
believed we were wonderfully clever

We looked hard in the mirror
at our 12-year-old faces
searching for likeness
decided our mouths were both Russian
vowed never to marry any of the sons
of our parents' friends

I got married to a dental student

You went away to live with your mother

I heard you had a husband and a baby boy

Saw a snapshot of your son

on the steps of your quiet life

I left the dentist, got my degree

Years and years have passed

We see each other never

What of our childhood then?

Now I have two girls, the oldest has

cerebral palsy: it has changed my life

She has taught me to see new colors in a rainbow

and that there are no answers to my questions

Your aunt Muriel hates my hippy life

My aunt Esther is dead of breast cancer

My youngest, when she smiles

I see she has a Russian mouth

Finding Crumbs

Free Time

Just made matzoh balls for soup.

Gone for a few hours are

the four small hands that always

make them with me.

Gone too are the grown-up hands

that made the chicken soup.

First time alone in the house

for a long long time.

I'll do some writing

from words in an old notebook

left over from my first marriage,

it's red, once had recipes in it.

There's scribbling on a yellowed page

where a glued-in clipping from a magazine

has fallen off,

leaving only the handwritten title:

Porcupine meatballs.

Finding Crumbs

When you were seven
and said we should enjoy
every crumb
of every minute
of every day,

you didn't know
there would be minutes, days
too terrible to enjoy
too dark to find even crumbs.

But still
somehow
that young spirit
endures.

To Anna, Nearly Thirteen

We're watching the State of the Union
Look at the Supreme Court, I say
I'm watching the President, you answer
That's what I want to be

    Helen Caldicott

    said on the radio

    that 75 percent

    of your generation

    think you won't

    grow up

Your hard shattering footsteps
drive rainbows into the air
tell the earth you are here

    When you were very young

    and always at my side, you said,

    I want to die when you die

    No, I said, *you will not want that*

Now you eye me carefully, critically

hatefully even

and I can smile, because everything

always changes

From your bed you shout *oooooh*

there's a big black spider in here!

but you pick it up

with a Kleenex

place it out the window

alive

She said, on the radio

that we should tell our children

what we're going to do

to save

the world

The Day My Daughter Stayed Home
Because She Was Bitten by a Mosquito

Anna screeched into the mirror

My God! Look at my lip!

So I looked at her lip

and saw her

looking at me looking at her lip

We held back a moment

then broke out laughing

A good excuse for a day off, she said

Yes, I agreed, and called the school—

Alas, the flu

We planned a day of bookstores

the library, lunch with grandma

Oh, the wonders of the human body—

The lip was down to normal

as we finished off our breakfast

Together we walked through streets

wet with last night's rain

She kept looking at the top of my head

to see if she was taller yet

Two Mothers with "Different" Children

We have laughed together
But Valerie, one night we cried
as our partners watched
with their dry men's eyes

We cried for our children
their struggles and hurts
You said it was the first time
in a long time
But I have done it often

Oh, I also get angry
talk to teachers, write letters
But I laugh too
and say to her, my daughter,
who has a wonderful laugh,
We don't have to take this seriously,
do we?

But one night we cried, Valerie

His pain, hers

It is there in us

We saw it in each other

University Applications

Searching through papers

asking questions

my two eager daughters and I

try to fit our whole lives

into the narrow lines

of their application forms.

There is no category for my occupation

or space to explain a lifestyle.

When exactly was the divorce,

Girl Scout camp, math contest

and what *will* I earn this year?

I sort through memories for answers

try to imagine

this table, this house

without them.

Questions

When I was born
did you have any idea
what my life would be like?
She's home from college,
a respite from roommate problems

My tears in the shower are hidden
while long-buried what-ifs emerge
Whose fault was it anyway?
The answer to her question, of course,
is no

Is your life, in general, good?
She considers, then answers:
Given society's attitudes
toward people with disabilities
I'm living the best possible life

The End of Something

One calls, the other faxes
I might not be home for Grandma's birthday
She needs to prepare eight hundred images
for the website launching
This is how start-ups are, mom
Her first check, after two weeks
matches my monthly one

The other sends me two short stories
she wants to publish, seeks my opinion
I marvel at her wisdom,
the tragic, tender prose
She is, yes, a better writer than I
who sit with my Irish whiskey
in the empty house

Logic

Look, I say, pointing to a balloon-strewn sign

proclaiming "Claire and Audrey"

A lesbian commitment ceremony

right here on my road   Cool!

Maybe they're twins, my daughter says

What?

Having their birthday

Well, I shoot back

I suppose they could be cousins

or even friends born the same day

or a girl and her grandma

You could see if the sign's there

next year, she tells me

But the grandma could be visiting

from Scotland just this once

or the friend could die

If it's not there, she says

then maybe it is a lesbian wedding

My Daughter at Twenty-two

Tall cliffs of coastal fog,
pelicans in formation,
an occasional maverick seagull
as I drive north on Highway One

Visits are rare
with this girl on her own,
the cord stretched taut
before the break

She has worn herself out
so we spend the afternoon
sitting at her round blue table
drinking tea, catching up

Later we walk, arm in arm,
eat tacos, laugh
She is glad I am visiting
I cannot get enough of her

She asks me not to come

to the play she's in,

I'll make her nervous

But please yes please do come

when she has four teeth pulled,

the ones they call wisdom

Capitola Morning

She opens her red curtains
smiles at the fog

Puts on her sweats
goes down by the river
stares at the mist on the water
takes it all in
the quiet and softness

When she can pull away
from the river fog
she walks down to bask
in ocean fog, which, to her
is the perfect morning place

She stands on the pier
surrounded by gray
Thick, peaceful gray

Fog changes an everyday landscape
into a fairyland
Erases all the hard edges

Another Capitola Morning

A white dove picks at breadcrumbs I've brought
as I watch a heron, still as stars.
The mother duck with the sixteen babies
is missing today.

Swallows and their shadows
flutter against cliffs,
hover at the mounds of their nests,
dart over waves and back again
making a circular ceiling above me.

Pigeons search for strands of seaweed
for eggs to rest on
underneath the pier,
the feet of fishermen
just inches away.

I pull my troubles
from their hiding places,
arrange them on the horizon
to be separated and scrutinized.

But the wheels of my brain
are stuck in sand.
I can only watch the ocean,
breathe in the fog.

Off-Season in Capitola Village

An old man is doing Tai Chi
knees bent, hands just so
next to driftwood sculptures
he might have created

He faces the sea, his bald circle
bright in the morning sun
Long white hair
flowing from the edges

Teen-aged surfers test themselves
in the diamond-flecked water
A woman sits on a bench, smoking
And because it's Monday,
a garbage truck beeps in the road

La Traviata will be here in the Spring
as tourists begin their annual migration
Soon my kayak will be launched
in the green and quiet creekway

What I Might Tell Anna

Besides raising the wonder

of every precious sense

especially *touch*

and providing me with curious

thoughts to ponder,

   for example: *You can die in any kind of way*

         and then it becomes a story to be told

               and you won't know anything about it

marijuana does these two things

      It slows me down

      letting me communicate better

      with Becky,

      It blunts the world outside

      and how it treats her

Last Eggs

Fifty

Before work I stack wood

wash floors

for my parents

After work I go dancing

with my daughter

till midnight

Soon, everything will change

Kalalau Blood

I sit in a pool
with a waterfall
watch the blood
and the river
blend

My first time
letting myself bleed
and bleed
no tampons
no pads
or sponge
no stopping
the bright dark blood
or the river

I stand
stretch to the sun
its warmth on my breasts
taking in birdsong
and the scent
of yellow plumeria

Identical Windows

Days before the long-planned gathering
our cousin Carol died, not unexpectedly
but at an unexpected time

Let's go, I tell my brother
We should attend the funeral
But there's still so much to do
to get his place reunion-ready
I'll come down and help, I say
Whatever needs doing

The windows, he says, all of them, like this
He demonstrates his method, it takes me all day
Through the glass I see him
cleaning the yard, leaving for the dump
I imagine how in a few days
so many relatives will be here
Cousins, raised to be close, coming from far away,
our children, our children's children

At the funeral Carol's identical twin

speaks of a closeness we can't imagine

She is the first of us to die

Back home, I read her recent emails

then wash my own windows

using my brother's newspaper

and warm soapy water method

To PDX

I buckle myself into the coveted
window seat, a few rows down
definitely in front of the wing
for best viewing

Snow below, in squares
How does that happen?
Like a patchwork quilt
on an unmade bed

Mt Shasta looms suddenly
and I search for skiers,
climbers, anyone
visible in the distance

Rims of a hundred old volcanoes
outlined in white
as we speed toward the greatest of all:
Crater Lake, and memories flood in

I am standing on its edge

a kid on a camping trip

staring into blue

trying to fathom the depth

The Sisters reach upward

then Mt Hood, Mt Jefferson

and, finally, with its top blown off

Mount St Helens

Manhattan Lunch

The door opens and my ears are assaulted
by the jackhammer destroying the sidewalk.
An old woman takes so long coming in
the blasting sound pierces people at their tables,
jolts the food behind the counter.

She wears a scarf that is hardly there
and a grey coat considerably torn,
slowly looks the place over,
chooses a table next to mine.
She looks in the direction of the food,
starts counting
pennies   nickels   dimes
pulled from the corners of her pockets.

I stand to get another cup of coffee,
bend down to her.
Do you want something to eat?
No, I'm just counting my money. See?
She smiles at me.
I have a lot.

Last Eggs

Tiny bottles of colored powders
stand on shelves along the walls.
A sweet cinnamon smell wafts
through rosy light.
Smiling fetuses float in glass bowls
waiting to be lifted and held.

Wise and ancient women are busy
measuring, mixing, weighing, feeding.
You can have a baby too, they tell me.
Oh no, I've hardly any eggs left
and those that are, well, they're old.
The women laugh gently: it's very easy,
these herbs will bring everything back.
Oh no, I say again, I've already had
my children, they're nearly grown and gone.
We will take care of you, they chant,
we will take care of the baby.

And then my body remembers the wonder.
Remembers how precious
the births and babies were.
Yes, I say to the women, yes.

Awake the next morning
the once familiar
sticky mucus of ovulation
stretches between my fingers.

Thoughts on an Airplane Two Days Before My 58th Birthday

Why, on every flight

is my gate always the last one

down the long airport concourse?

I must tell Anna I have a row all to myself

just as we joked about last night in the restaurant

I can't get any work done because of the view,

would almost pay the fare just to see the world from here

I arrived in L.A. minutes before she walked through customs

into my waiting arms

We stretched out on the hotel bed

talking, laughing

looking at her photos of the South Pacific

She brought me gifts:

New Zealand chocolate

A Booker-prize novel by an author she met

Miniature bottle of Johnnie Walker, string of tiny shells

she made sitting on a beach in Fiji

In the morning, I watched her plane taxi out of sight

soon to be in the heart of yet another country

Looking down at the mountains,

I wonder, is it earthquakes

that make their layers

visible from the top?

They say when a volcano

erupts beneath the ocean

it shoots a wall of black water

straight up into the sky

I always look for this

when flying to Hawaii

I think of W, our nights together

soaring higher and higher

into another world

We are about to fly right into thunder

Exclamation Points

Long Live the Difference

It seems the woman's chromosome

the one they call X

scatters, untraceable

spreads helter-skelter

in her children.

All the better for survival.

The man's, that Y

goes straight to the son

unchanged.

And by tracking this

we know that Africans

fleeing drought

walked all the way to Australia

populating the earth

evolving as necessary.

Trincas

My grandchild grows ripe
in the belly of my daughter
and I have some questions

How might this change
our unpredictable relationship
and will I be a grandmother
my daughter approves of

(The name I made up
from the ones
she's considering
was not a source
of amusement)

How long might I have
to watch it grow
in the world—
this newest person
on a list, a very long list

going back to the beginning

of humanity itself

Oh Brandy Leave Me Alone

These are unlikely words for a lullaby
but I used to sing them to my girls
because I loved the melody,
a song I heard many times
as a child myself,
on an old record of my parents'
called *Songs of the South African Veld*.

Not long ago
I sang it to my grandson
as I caught my daughter
glance at her husband
whom she had told that brandy
wasn't the only thing about me
she disapproved of.
But she looked at me and smiled
and the baby fell asleep.

Then one night
engrossed in *The New Yorker*

and listening to Larry Kelp on KPFA

out of the corner of my ear

I heard the familiar melody

and called him up, long distance,

but he was too busy to talk.

I know how that is

from my days as a disk jockey.

He did announce

that many had called him

about the old Pete Seeger collection

so he read off all the songs

including *Brandy Leave Me Alone.*

The next day I googled it.

The original words are in Afrikaans.

It can be taken as a love song

or a cry for deliverance from alcohol.

It really isn't a lullaby at all.

Nearly Three

"I want the baby to have MY name,"
Lukas tells his mother
(never mind that it might be a girl)
"and I'll be JAMES!"

"Let's put long pants on today,"
my daughter tells him.
"No."
 He is enamored with skateboarding
and those guys wear shorts.
"You'll want to wear them soon, honey,
it's getting chilly."
"No."
"Well, let's cross that bridge
when we get to it,"
she tells him.
"Let's cross that CHILLY bridge?"
he asks, and later, as they
pull up to his pre-school:
"Is this that chilly bridge?"

And later still:

"I'm not honey. Are you going

to put me in your tea?"

He asks her why some boys' penises

are smaller than his.

"It's probably because

they are circumcised," she says,

not going into detail.

Later, in public, he points to

a small tricycle and says loudly,

"Mommy, look at the circumcised tricycle!"

Once home, she explains that the word

applies only to penises.

Cross-Country Conversation
with a Three-Year-Old

"Grammy! I have the *chicken* things

... the chicken *cups*."

"Pox," my daughter says in the background,

"you have the chicken *pox*."

Lukas giggles.

"I don't *know* this word," he says.

Two days later

it's snowing there.

"Grammy, it's a *disaster* here!"

"Why is it a disaster?" I ask

"I don't *know* why it's a disaster."

"Why do you *say* it's a disaster?"

"I say it because it *is* a disaster!"

When we hang up

I think about language and grandsons,

daughters and disasters.

The Little Pretend Park

For Lukas, going on 4

Tied to the oak tree

the old hammock swing

carries him high,

my foot pushing

as I lie on the chaise

He's here, finally, from New York

seeing the redwoods and fog,

my house with the mailbox down the road,

his family in California

This is the life, I say to him

This is the life, he answers back

This is the LIFE, he shouts

throwing his arms in the air

New York Week

We drop my daughter off to catch a train to Astoria,
her boys in their car seats.
Orion is sad, Lukas says when she's gone,
because the num-nums are dancing away.
I laugh out loud at Lukas' description of his brother's
deprivation of breast milk and try to cheer them up
by singing "Lovely Rita Meter Maid," which
I can hardly remember but they think is very funny.

I go Greek dancing with Katherine,
my son-in-law's mother,
a relationship for which there is no name
in English, but in Greek there is.

Much of my time is spent with Lukas.
We play cowboys with lariats,
fish from our kayak-bed,
build miniature cities, wink at each other
over his joke about "suffering"
and make up stories.

We go to the playground even though it is dark

and everything is wet.

He tells me about cars,

I tell him about airplanes.

He cries when I leave, but when I call

later, it is snowing in New York

and that, he tells me, is a thing he loves.

Flying home, I watch the sunset for hours,

think about my favorite times:

Lukas scrambling into my bed every morning

    for a snuggle,

Orion rushing up with lips pursed for a kiss.

Their father telling me he definitely wants them all

to come to California again next summer.

My daughter saying she's glad I'm there.

Saying it more than once.

Exclamation Points

I am visiting for their birthdays

Two & Five

October days filled with music,

remote-control cars, learning to write.

And Halloween.

Lukas and I compose a song,

he on his new piano keyboard

and I on Orion's ukulele.

He does the words, I the tune.

One Halloween in Port Washington

a famous band played at a wedding

They played so good that the people gave them candy

and they danced half the night till the sun came up

They played so good that they played the next night

at a big Italian wedding

And the bride told a joke

(*glissando* on the piano with a flourish & a grin!)

What is 8 plus a cow?
No one knew the answer
but the cat took a bow

Hours are spent at the kitchen table,
Lukas' mouth scrunched in concentration
as he prints capital letters at random
then laughs when I tell him what they spell.

He is fascinated by symbols:
Question mark, exclamation point, and dot dot dot.
He thinks it's terrific there's a sign
for something exciting and important
or when you don't finish your sentence.

Later, getting ready for bed,
he shouts out: *Grammy, come here!*
Look! He points to his sheets
covered in trucks & cars & exclamation points:
Beep! Beep! Honk! Honk!
He tells me: *This is really important!*

Once home, my daughter calls.

They all had the stomach flu

but laughed through it anyway

because throwing up

was dubbed *Big Spit!* by Orion.

And Lukas sends me his first letter

written without parental assistance.

On one side: *Grammy.*

On the other, pictures and words:

Team and *Ship* and, really important, *Airplane!*

The No-Training-Wheels Revolution

Orion was the first
to go big time,
fueled by the falling-off
of one training wheel.

"It's time!" my daughter declared,
removing the remaining balancing device.
At three-and-a-half, he ventured
precariously into the street
with a steadying hand and advice
from parents and big brother
on the importance of starting
with one pedal up.

Well! The four-year-old next door
was soon heard imploring his dad
to remove those baby things.
And the six-year-old on the other side
absolutely needed hers dismantled.

Now the neighborhood
is training-wheel free,
except for the two-year-old
who watches and waits,
longing to get bigger.

Park Anywhere

My grandson at five was fascinated

with Becky's disability placard.

We could park close to entrances

at many colors of curbs

and never have to pay.

Did you buy it? Do they just send it to you?

I told him it was because she walks with crutches.

Oh, I thought it was just random.

We gave him an expired one

which he put on a wagon

said now he could park it anywhere.

Sidewalks of Santa Fe

One moment we were walking, talking, waving our arms.
The next I was slammed face-down on the pavement,
tripped on an unseen hazard.
My grandson, shocked as I was,
wondered why I didn't get right up,
but I was in a fog, feeling for broken teeth.

The black eyes and bruises worsened by the hour
as the humor grew bolder.
You're going to scare little children when you go home
said one grandson.
You could cover your face with band-aids
or better yet, wear a mask
said the other, laughing hilariously.
In the end I borrowed his sunglasses
with instructions not to take them off
under any circumstances
although I had to when the TSA official insisted
I need to see your eyes.

Once in the air, I removed the glasses,

told the woman next to me

I had to be onstage in two weeks.

There's always make-up, she said

or you could write a poem.

Which I did, on the back of a shopping list.

Please, take a bigger piece of paper

and she tore one out of her sketchbook.

The flight attendant looked at me knowingly,

piled my tray with packets of honey-roasted peanuts.

Perfect Timing

Sex

A Jamaican taught me how good it is

A New Yorker showed me how much fun

A cowboy taught me how sad it can be

And a Jew, he took me to the depths of the universe

    and I have his children

But the musician keeps it golden

    after all these years

Time Travel

I never stopped loving you, he says
squeezing my hand in both of his
Stunned, I close my eyes
let the memories come
searching for reasons why
I stayed so long

He says he is sorry
for all the awful things
he's done
You should be, I tell him
wondering which awful things
he means

I am, he says, his eyes seeking
a way back in
But I am cool and leave him hungry

Later, making love with another
I did get them mixed up

There were, after all

a few good reasons

Finally

Two children

Three miscarriages

Thousands of orgasms

And half as many heartaches

There was passion

There was meanness

There was laughter

And adventure

Inevitably it ended

But love, even ruined, is not easily erased

From our changed and distant lives

We tried to reach one another

Until now

Tuesday Night

I stroke and stare

at the cat

Fire snaps behind him

Eyes closed but

I see body-flicks

ear-twitches

Not sure he trusts

the fire?

Listening

for someone outside?

We both

wait

Still Life

The half-burnt candle

casts giant shadows of lily and iris

from the vase of fading flowers

taller than the globe

spun to Africa

A near-empty bottle of Jack Daniel's

two shot glasses without a drop

an empty pipe

ashtray from Mexico

condom wrapper and Astroglide

And Paco de Lucia on repeat

as I fall into a Flamenco dream

Sostenuto*

After he leaves

she floats down the stairs

turns off the music

the red chili lights

the heat

breaks off a square

of fine dark chocolate

lets it melt on her tongue

Musical term meaning to sustain or prolong a note.

The Golden Years

I can see it now,

I tell him the next morning,

Local woman dies

after world's longest orgasm.

You laugh and say it wouldn't be

such a bad way to....

Not yet, I interrupt, not yet.

Who would have thought

after all these years

there would be so much gold?

Perfect Timing

There comes a point
when you can't stop
even if a tree falls in the forest
and anyway, the earth
is already moving

Turns out a tree did fall
crashed slowly, noisily
taking out smaller ones
somewhere near the house

We lay for a long time
holding tight while
our heartbeats slowed
senses returned to normal

Finally you said,
"Did you hear...?"
And we laughed
and we laughed

Holding On

From Dad

He gave me his zoom lens
He didn't
really want to
My mother
said did you
give it to her
Not yet he said
Well she said
to me
it's too heavy for him to
lift anymore

I said he could have it
back when he wanted
He didn't say anything
She looked at me
I said thanks I really
like it

Fire Season

My brother and I do this

for her, our mother

He lifts the split wood

into the wheelbarrow

I stack it in the shed

leaving no spaces between

She sits among the trees

in a white chair

and talks to us of our father

while my daughter helps us

handing me the logs one by one

our gloved hands working together

Later we bring more chairs

admire our work, praise his woodshed

We talk carefully, lovingly about him

and sometimes we laugh

His absence hurts us all

Not long ago on the other side

of the big redwood where we sit

we put his ashes in the ground

near those of his mother

poured Old Taylor whiskey

slowly over the top

then drank the rest ourselves

The time since he died

is full of things I want to tell him

February Light

For my father

So much about you was summer

Your birthdate on the solstice

Your death in July many years ago

The hot sun of your New Mexico boyhood

Your love of the long-light days

when in the hours after work

you built your home among the redwoods

But it is late in winter

that memories of you stir

when I see the yellow daffodils

you planted long ago

bloom for another generation, another

and yet another

alongside this house

where I live now

Slow Learner

I was 43

before

I realized

my mother likes

to be called

Annie

not *Anne*

And

it wasn't much

before that

when

I realized I

was not

her best friend

Ma

I spend the evening with her
We drink Irish whiskey
That's her thing
and I like it too

We talk about her loneliness
Old friends gone
The people who don't call
since Dad died

We laugh too
and the dinner's nice
I drive home carefully
watch for deer

I light my pipe
That's my thing
I think of her life
I think of mine

To My Mother, With One Breast

Sitting with a margarita

alone on the balcony

after the storm

I watch the waves for hours

Huge, steamy, wonderfully curved

I want to bring you here

to cheer you up

have a few

I telephone

No, you say, too soon

After my third drink

I tell the waitress

She smiles into the fog

Says she would have them both removed

My child's eye sees you naked

Breasts full

Hair black, curly

So plentiful we had jokes about it

And laughing, you taught me

to love my body too

We don't yet know

the extent of your cancer

I would give both my breasts

to keep you

here

Eightieth Birthday Gift

For my mother

Four o'clock in the morning
Mosquitoes keeping me awake
Orion with the moon above his shoulder
floats slowly across the sky

Lights flicker in Albania
distant and grey
Too early for the boat from Brindisi
but not the Athens-bound airplane

Dogs, roosters, birds
announce the day
Not a single human sound
save one: my mother snoring

A string of brightness
crosses the island
from our village to Corfu Town
I stand on the balcony

in my new Italian nightgown

marveling at this voyage

the two of us have made

Corfu

Olive branches sway
obscuring distant lights
The sunset is finished
two ouzos, as well

I sit here, the highest point
and call out hello to Ian
a new friend, here for a week

Unexplained fireworks pop in the night
The waitress hasn't a clue
Maybe a celebration, she says

Soon I'll be wending my way
to the hotel, in the dark
but it'll be nothing like the book
my daughter gave me to read
How Late It Is, How Late
about blindness, and loneliness

Holding On

It was quite a number of hours

and late into the night

that my brothers and I

sat around the fire

the day our mother died

before pouring ourselves a drink

a small one at that

It was quite a number of weeks

after moving into her house

her spirit everywhere

before I would get high, alone

Daughters & Mothers

Next weekend I'm going to Berkeley
and to Sacramento the one after
my daughter tells me
as we drive up Highway One
She waits
That's good, I say
You'll be all right? she asks

Are you coming home every weekend
because you think I'm not okay?
Yes
I really am fine now, I tell her
You can have your own life back
She looks at me and grins

For a month before my mother died
I slept in my clothes, I slept a lot
Ate the same thing every day
Somehow I went to work
Somehow I took care of her

Something in me knew

what I didn't want to see

It has been three months

since the celebration of her life

I still start to phone her

I still cry at any time

But I'm all right now

The Clothes

It was months
before I could move them
from the shelves into plastic bags.
The two black bundles remained in the closet
until finally I could touch and sort through
her things, still carrying her smell and shape,
and now they're in the trunk of my car.

She would have wanted them
to go to a safe house for women
but they are not accepting any
due to lack of space.

Next I sought the homeless shelter,
comparing my scribbled address
with those on the houses
but could not find it.

The thrift store where I bought
so many children's clothes

would be a fitting place

for those of their grandmother

but the streets were crowded—

I could not park, took that as a sign.

So they are with me

in my car

everywhere I go.

Six Months Later

It started with a letter
from a friend of my mother
Had I received the plant she sent,
not that she was asking for a thank-you
Oh god I never finished writing them
Only did half, it was just too hard

But now, once more,
I get out the box
with all the written outpourings
since her death
Yes, I answered, it's planted by the front door
waiting to bloom this coming spring

Later I take some Irish whiskey,
sit near the buried ashes of my parents
wishing I believed
they were together now
with their own mothers, even

Grief takes over the day
There's nothing to do but let it

Don't Forget

Legacy

It comes with the hazel eyes

and all the hair

so the biopsy order

was not a shock

I have five working days to wonder

if this will be the one and only

the first of many

or nothing at all

Five working days

of panic and denial

imagining myself not here

less here

tentatively here

Five working days to pretend

nothing is amiss

because to tell it

makes it real

I thought I'd talk about it

with my old friend one night

but there's a power

in the not-telling

and everything he said to me

was heard with different ears

Prelude

I have ten thousand black dots

and one squiggly fish

swimming in my left eye

Oh and did I mention

the flashing lights?

It can happen with age

said the doc and the Internet

or from a blow to the head

which I did not have

So I stayed up one night

finished an entire bottle

of old vine Zinfandel

knowing I'm heading into

this reversed adolescence

a preface to being old

Why I Stopped Flying Lessons

There was the thing with my shoulders
both of them, boat injuries, no strength now
And the dizziness, only once
Just loose calcium in my ear
Can happen as you age they say
but would not want to be flying
if it happened again

Then there was the cost
So much money for my fun
And the stem cell treatments for Becky
would cost thousands
if we decided on that

Oh and the age thing
Wasn't as if I'd been flying for years
It was one of three things I wanted to do in my sixties
along with making wine and acting in a play
which I did

And the planes, they were old
Even my instructor needed pliers
for some of the knobs
What really settled it, though
were the two accidents:
First, the owner of the school
and his son, bad weather
Then a student and his instructor
in the mountains
All dead

But how I loved flying
If they're looking for an old gal
to fly into space
I'm here

Tuesday's Obituaries

I started reading them for familiar names

from a San Francisco childhood.

A fellow fourth grader who died too young,

perhaps a friend's mom whose secrets I knew

But now I'm fascinated

by these mini bios of ordinary lives.

A perfect dad,

the famous chef of Tarantino's,

the fellow who spent his retirement

fixing old radios

Caledonia "Sally" Calimquim Fernandez

Alexander "Ivan" Ivashkevich

Elisabeth Gloria (Marmit) Ohlendorf

The more accomplished are at the top:

a pilot/minister who died in Anchorage,

the Manhattan writer of children's books,

a spokeswoman for nursing home reform

Their stories told on a single day

Section C, page nine

On Thinking That I Must Go Hear
Adrienne Rich Next Monday

My dear friend Cathryn,

so lovely, so good,

smiled and told me

she had faced her death

It happened so fast,

aggressive, they said

Her mom Doris was there too

for a last goodbye

I crave poetry now,

the way it connects

in secret ways

like lasers through labyrinths

to things you know but

never hear about

Graduate School

They played that old Phil Ochs song

—*Changes*—

on the radio last night.

Put me back to New Jersey

and sweet Larry Schwartz.

He used to sit on the bed

with his guitar

and sing it to me.

We are seventy-something now.

Did he have a good life?

Did he have children?

Does he remember?

On My Brothers' Retirement

Toss out alarm clocks, lunchboxes,
the number to call
when you're sick or whatever.
Here's to the greatest of times,
to the best of brothers.

I pushed Johnny in a stroller
hoping people didn't think
he was actually my baby.
Terry, much closer in age,
shares my childhood
as no other person can:
the meetings, the FBI,
Dad's accident.

Every time we talk, you both
show me the gentleness of men,
the caring of brothers.
We visit for the fun of it
take vacations together

and after all these years
we're still sharing the pipe.

Now we enter new territory
not always easy, as we have seen.
Years from now
I hope we look back
at all the good things
that happened after today.

The Day After the Election, 2016

Pulling up to the curb to let my daughter out,

the ticket-lady got out of her little white car

waving her arms at me.

I'm just dropping her off! She's disabled! She lives here!

I didn't need to shout.

Calm down. I just want to point out a place especially for that.

Taking a deep breath, I looked at her. Her face fell.

I'm so sad today she said.

Me too. We both started crying.

She leaned in through my window and gave me a long hug.

Then went behind the car and hugged my daughter.

What's your name? I'm Ruth. I've seen you around here.

I waved good-bye to both of them

and drove home the long way

so I could see the ocean.

Don't Forget

First they say you do
and then you don't
And then they say you do
have uterine cancer

Friends email support
beginning with *oh shit*

I expected breast cancer
like my mom, my brilliant radical aunt
and their mother, dead before I was born

But I feel fine
Becky's trust is set up
Anna gets the rest
I'm trying to declutter
That'll be a good thing
when I'm still here later

Forget Weight Watchers for now

Forget going to the gym

Don't forget Tuesday nights

Savor everything

Be glad you were born

Be very very glad

"I'm Sorry About Your Orgasms"

My doctor looked sincere
and, I think, a little amused
We did this to you

The uterus had to come out
of this there was no question
but apparently its contractions
had something to do with
those long and lovely orgasms

But the cancer is gone
she said, eyebrows hopeful
Yes, I said, *it's gone*

Chatterbox Falls

Princess Louisa Inlet, BC

I didn't think the name was fitting

for something so magnificent,

the eighth wonder of the world, some say.

In what is known as the boaters' bible

Erle Stanley Gardner is quoted:

Perhaps an atheist could view it and

remain an atheist, but I doubt it.

I hiked as close as I could

over rocks and fallen trees

to watch the water's incredible force

as it crashed onto rocks,

dissolved into billows of lacey mist.

I cried at the beauty

I thought about time.

The few boaters there were also surprising.

The man on *Melody* had a piano on board,

played musicals while we stood on the small dock
  with our drinks.
The couple on *Serenity* said their daughter and I work at
  the same college!
And the woman who docked closest to the roaring falls
  told us
I'm from Berkeley and I am still an atheist.

2020 Vision

Everything stopped around my birthday,

celebrated on FaceTime with whiskey and friends

There was the memorial I missed in Eugene,

a dear friend from the '60s

and two graduations in Santa Fe—

A daughter getting her Master's

A grandson finishing high school

What might his generation do

to forge a new world—

healthcare, housing, justice for all

Zoom is our connection now

Hiking group, writing group, family every Sunday

friends in England, yoga, concerts and cocktails

I buy soy creamer for my neighbor

She gives me fresh eggs

which I use in the crepes

made from sourdough starter

that we have with blueberries

nearly every morning

There've been mix-ups with the vegetable deliveries,

strange technical difficulties with phone and computer

and some animal dancing on the roof at night

I've had two ticks on my back

two crowns off my teeth

Haven't seen my lover in months

and now he has prostate cancer

Every morning my daughter and I do the NYT crossword

and discuss how we would answer the advice column

We find tiny yellow flowers never before noticed

on daily walks to fetch newspaper and mail

wearing whatever, no bra, wild hair

At night we watch Rachel to keep informed

then Colbert, Trevor Noah, and movies

I weed-whack and stack firewood

publish monthly newsletters for state retirees

shop every two weeks during senior hour

work on my book of poems

worry about what's next

About the Author

Dena Taylor is retired from careers in education and social work. She is the co-author, with Becky Taylor, of *Tell Me the Number Before Infinity: the story of a girl with a quirky mind, an eccentric family, and oh yes, a disability,* and the author, editor, or co-editor of six books on women's issues. She lives in Northern California.

Colophon

Printer, poet, editor and book designer Kate Hitt established Many Names Press in 1993 to address the need by literary writers and artists to broadcast their exemplary works through a small press. Some of the esteemed poets and writers she has published are: Louise Grassi Whitney, Eli Whitney, Becky Taylor, Dena Taylor, Douglas McClellan, Barbara Leon, Herme Medley, Maude Meehan, Clair Killen, Margarite Tuchardt, Amber Coverdale Sumrall, Adrienne Rich (memorial broadside) and Patrice Vecchione.

Exclamation Points uses Jan Tschichold's *Sabon* for the text, with Eric Spiekermann's *Berliner Grotesque* in the titling.

CPSIA information can be obtained
at www.ICGtesting.com
Printed in the USA
LVHW011155190820
663480LV00006B/351